The Home Concepts Extensions & Conversions Book

First Edition

The Home
Concepts
Extensions & Conversions Book

First Edition

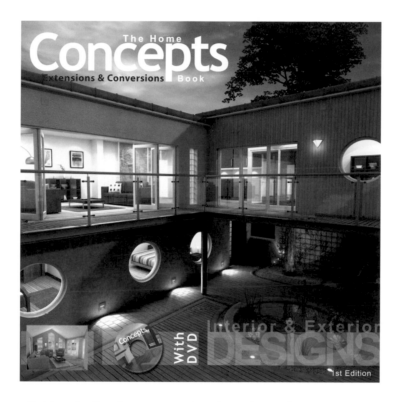

Essential inspiration for anyone planning a home improvement project

Written by

L.Byrne

Paul Molloy

with 3D visuals by

Pixelbrick

SHORELINE
PRESS

Printed and bound by:
Standard Printers
Ballybrit Ind Est
Ballybrit
Galway
Rep. of Ireland

www.standardprinters.ie

Published by:
Shoreline Press
Fifth Floor
121 Capel Street
Dublin 1
Rep. of Ireland

Tel: +353 1 8733568
Fax: +353 1 8733568

www.shorelinepress.ie

First published in 2008

ISBN: 9780955014529

Text copyright © Shoreline Press Ltd 2008

Design, visuals and photographs copyright © Pixelbrick 2008

Designs by Lesley R Hutt & Partners
Roger Parry & Associates
Mexlib Design
Dominic Whoriskey
Mezzanine Architectural Services
Ivory Architects
JP Timber Construction

Contents

Introduction

Over time our domestic needs may change and demand extra living space. Extending or converting part of your property provides the perfect solution when your house can no longer accommodate.

Generally less costly and disruptive than a move, a house extension or conversion allows you to remain in the home and area you love whilst gaining on living space and hopefully adding value to your property. With house prices falling or static, the trend towards home extensions and conversions is on the increase with more and more people looking to upsize their property rather than face the tumultuous task of relocating.

There are numerous options open to homeowners looking for more living space – whether it's making use of surrounding land to extend a home, or transforming an empty attic space into a beautiful rooftop retreat, there is nearly always a way to enhance your property.

If you are one of the thousands of people each year who want to improve and not move, then The Home Concepts Book *Extensions and Conversions* has a host of exciting designs to inspire new and develop existing ideas on making the most of your home. The designs and information inside have been put together to help motivate and assist anyone through the process, with information also included on design, planning requirements, hiring professional help, landscaping and eco-considerations.

User guide and notes

The designs inside have been created by respected architects & home designers from the UK and Ireland and are intended to inspire and fuel your imagination. You may find aspects within the various designs that when combined create a unique plan that fulfils your requirements. Alternatively you may fall for one of the extensions exactly as it is shown, in which case you can contact the architect listed inside to discuss in more depth. General information and a recommended reading and website guide are located at the back of the book. All room and house sizes featured in The Home Concepts Book *Extensions and Conversions* are approximate.

DVD

The DVD is suitable for playing on most home DVD players and PC and Mac computers with DVD playing software installed.

The Design Stage

Adding space to a treasured home can be both rewarding and life enhancing. Be it an opportunity to expand your property with a growing family or tailoring a house to suit your lifestyle, the options are great.

One obvious advantage to extending or converting is that you avoid the unsettling and expensive experience of moving house, although carrying out construction work on your existing property will certainly impact on your daily life in the short term. Building work is a messy business and there will be dust, rubble and building materials to contend with. Often areas of your home will be uninhabitable during the work and you may have to find alternative accommodation while the extension is being built, which can be a daunting prospect for young or large families and is an added expense to be accounted for. Depending on your financial situation and level of trust with your project manager/builder, you may even decide to take a holiday while works are carried out

and leave things completely in the hands of the professionals. If you plan to stay in your home during construction and are hiring builders and tradesmen then the fact is you will be sharing your home with strangers for a substantial period of time, which can be stressful in itself.

Before a brick has been laid, there are a number of considerations to be thought through. Does your planned extension require planning permission? Are you up to speed on building regulations and how these will affect your plans? Are you going to draw the designs yourself or enlist the help of an architect or home designer? Are you going to attempt the construction yourself or source a builder for the majority or all of the work?

Ensuring that your extension can facilitate its intended use is vital. To get the most from a design it is worth contacting a qualified architect or architectural technician. These highly skilled professionals are trained to make the

most of available space and can put you on the right track in terms of what is and isn't feasible. The architect or technician can also assist in submitting your plans for planning permission and guide you on how to comply with building regulations. Again, such a service will take a slice from the overall build budget, so it is important to total up all the definite and potential expenses beforehand and make sure you have the funds to cover them. For more information on hiring a designer, see the Hiring a Professional section on page 25

The design of your home extension will be governed mainly by two factors; the size of the area available to build on and what it will be used for.

There could be any number of reasons why you want to extend. A growing family, need for a home office or larger kitchen, or maybe just to create more space and light. Whatever the motivation behind it, your extension needs to be designed with your end goal in mind. You must be certain that the space available is sufficient to

11

accommodate the function of the new building – bad planning and design will have a negative effect on the value of your property as a whole.

In terms of design, you should bear in mind the balance of your home – if you are extending to add bedrooms, you should increase the number of bathrooms to facilitate this. House buyers will expect at least one bathroom plus a shower room in a four or five bedroom property. Avoid having a bathroom only on the ground floor of a house – for the sake of practicality the bathroom should be easily accessible from the bedrooms and is a factor future homebuyers will consider.

If you are extending to facilitate a new dining area, work out the room needed for tables and chairs, and access to the bathroom/kitchen. It wouldn't be a very relaxing dinner party to have guests crammed into their seats and squeezing past each other to get to the bathroom! Think about how and when the new area will be used and design your plans accordingly. Depending on the planning

authority, there may be minimum room size restrictions in place designed to deter homeowners from cramming too many rooms into too small a space.

Adding extra room can also provide the perfect opportunity to completely transform the layout of your home – don't be afraid to go for a complete interior rearrangement if it means making the most of your extension.

The Mood/Style Board

Intended as visual source of inspiration, use a large board or scrap book to keep magazine cuttings, pictures, photographs, and anything relevant found in books or online. Interlace it with descriptive words and phrases based on the concept of your home extension. Focus on words that express how you see

Mood/Style Board

it – happy, warm, fresh – along with more functional requirements such as size and intended use.

Armed with a prioritised list and mood board, it will be much easier to communicate your requirements to an architect or house designer. The more an architect realises their client's expectations, the better positioned they are to create a successful design.

Enhancing your Home

An extension should mean just that – an extension of your existing home, not a separate entity stuck on the side or back that looks out of place with the rest of the house. This doesn't mean you can't be creative in your plans, but be mindful that the new building should marry well with the existing one – whether you match it exactly to the style of your house or use a different but complimentary design.

It's always a good idea to study a wide range of plans, from the traditional to the more out there – not all will suit your tastes and needs, but doing this will help inspire and motivate you when designing your extension.

Be aware, however, that unusual or extravagant extensions won't necessarily

bring added value to your property. In fact, as well as the additional cost, they could alienate future buyers and devalue your home.

Access to your new extension is a big consideration. Make sure you are not giving up more than you are gaining - there's no point dividing up a decent sized

room to provide access to a small extension.

You might also consider a conservatory extension, although UK Building Regulations require most conservatories be separated from the existing house by exterior doors. This style can leave the new space feeling somewhat cut off from the rest of the house and, unless the conservatory is large enough to work as a room in its own it can end up being an expensive, underused space.

Future Proofing

Think about the extension in the long-term. Future proofing is the ability of your home to stand the test of time, both aesthetically and literally and a carefully considered extension can prolong its functionality and worth.

If you are building extra space as a playroom for young children, can it be changed into a study or 'den' style room for them when they are older? Do you plan to build further extensions in the future and how will this build affect any home improvements made at a later date.

13

In terms of the actual construction, it is important to choose good quality, hard wearing building materials that can withstand the damaging effects of weathering. Beware of cheap materials that look impressive on first inspection – it is likely these will prove to be a false economy, dilapidating rapidly and requiring maintenance or replacement not long down the line. The benefits of thoroughly researching your materials cannot be underestimated and you will save time and money as a result.

Think about the finish – if you go for a painted render finish for the

House finishes: pebble dash, render, stone & brick

exterior walls, they will require painting every couple of years. On the other hand, being able to paint your walls gives you the option to change the colour and appearance of your extension, providing another way to freshen the look and update it in years to come.

Placing more power sockets, phone and

TV points than required in the new area gives you more freedom should you decide to change its use at a later stage. It also eliminates the annoying problem of not being able to restyle a room because the television can only be located in one area due to the arrangement of power and cable points.

There are many ways in which your home and extension may function in the future – no one knows what lies in store so far ahead, but it is worth carefully considering all the possibilities.

14

Further Considerations

Neighbours

It is a good, not to mention a courteous idea, to consult your neighbours before beginning any form of extension to your property. It will reduce the likelihood of future conflicts if they are agreeable to your plans from the start. Make sure your neighbours are happy with your plans and offer their consent to any access that may be required via their grounds during the building works. If your planned extension does require planning permission, your neighbours will be informed by the council although they are sure to appreciate advance notice from you in person.

The Right to Light

In most instances, the right to light issue is relevant in city centre locations where buildings are in close proximity. This may be an issue if your extension impedes on the light available to a neighbouring property, most commonly if your development obstructs a side window. In such cases the person affected can

An extension can block direct sunlight reaching an adjoining property

lodge their objection with the planning authority, which may affect your chances of planning approval. You should be aware that objections based on the right to light can still be made after planning permission has been granted and depending on how detrimental the effect is to their light source, your neighbour can seek financial compensation through the courts or in extreme cases, an injunction to prevent the build going ahead. This is just one reason why prior consultation is so important - be sure that anyone affected by the new construction is informed and agreeable before work begins. Further information on The Right to Light issue can be found on www.rics.org

Party Wall Act

A party wall is one you share with an adjacent property, and applies to terraced or semi-detached homes. In the UK, The Party Wall Act 1996 currently states that neighbours on adjoining boundaries must be given notice of any party wall changes, and their consent is required for works to go ahead. Notices to the adjoining homeowners must be served, acknowledged and in place one month before work commences. There is no similar act in Ireland at present, although consultation with your neighbours is recommended when planning construction work that relies on a shared wall. A downloadable copy of The Party Wall Act 1996 can be found at www.communities.gov.uk

Materials and Finishes

Design – When Less Is More

It isn't always the case that more space adds more value to your home. Badly designed, unsympathetic extensions can put a serious dent in your properties worth and will cost more again to put right. They will deter future house buyers and may even damage relations with neighbours.

As a rule it's best to be guided by the original design of the house and maintain the features and details which give it its distinctive character. Authentic details offer a subtle, refined look because they are intended to be there – there is a risk that obvious, modern additions will look out-of-character and garish. Consider the style, age and materials of the existing building carefully and use these as a guide to what will work best alongside your home.

Of course, you don't have to replicate the original, and with the help of a design professional there is enormous potential to create a beautiful, yet contrasting, extension that enhances the overall appearance of your home.

Materials

We are all more aware these days of the damaging environmental effect caused by mass manufacturing. Not only does the energy required to run a house impact on the earth's resources, so too do the methods used to construct building materials. It is possible however to limit the adverse effect of material manufacture by choosing eco-friendly and renewable alternatives that provide a more healthy home and environment. Consider the following as possible options for your extension or conversion and ethically enhance your home.

Glass: The obvious material when light is desired, glazed walls, doors and even ceilings offer a sleek, modern style and allow the outside to become part of the interior design. Its transparent quality allows natural light into a room, reducing the need for artificial light which in turn, cuts energy consumption. Glass is a resilient material and can be recycled many times over without losing clarity.

A relatively recent development in glass manufacture has been the creation of low-emmisivity (low-E) glass, which works by allowing light in while reflecting about 90 per cent of heat back out. This is achieved by coating the glass with ultra thin metal oxides which also help block harmful UV rays. The heat that passes through the glass is retained in the room, making low-E glass a good material for maintaining comfortable indoor temperatures in both summer and winter. Glass blocks can be used to create opaque light sources and work particularly well as part of a basement ceiling where privacy is still required.

Concrete: Often seen as cold and characterless, the use of concrete can actually create smooth clean lines and add to a stylish, contemporary look. It can be used in conjunction with more organic materials to soften its stark impact. It gives solid structural support and can take many variations of form. Concrete enjoys a high thermal mass that can be harnessed for heating and cooling in a room. It is moisture and insect resistant, resilient in

harsh weather conditions and does not need continual maintenance. On the downside, the manufacture of concrete does release significant levels of carbon dioxide into the atmosphere, although consumers can opt for honeycombed or lightweight concrete blocks to offset this process somewhat, or look into the availability of ecocement – produced using a zero-emission process from a combination of incineration ash, sewage sludge and additional limestone and clay.

Metal: Again, a material with a modern feel. Different types of metal, particularly steel, can be used in conjunction with concrete and glass to create an urban and industrialised look and also provide good, solid frameworks.

Environmentally speaking the energy used to produce metal is high and the pollution caused is significant. Also, the mining of metals can destroy natural habitats and wildlife. However, metals are recyclable, hard wearing and last for years. Salvage and scrapyards are a good place to look for reclaimed metal, especially when looking for unusual interior fittings. During construction, try to use bolted metal sections rather than those welded together in a structure so that they can be dismantled and reused at a later stage.

Wood: The connotations with warmth and homeliness are instinctive with wood, making it a popular choice as a building material. In these environmentally aware times much of the timber used in

construction comes from sustainable sources, and better still, the trees from which this versatile material derives naturally reduce levels of carbon dioxide in the atmosphere making it very much an

eco-friendly option. Be sure however to check the timber you use is from a sustainable source – many hardwood forests have been decimated by relentless logging, and the 'slash and burn' technique of felling and burning huge sections of South American rainforest is responsible for releasing vast quantities of carbon dioxide into the air. As well as contributing to climate change, mass deforestation also causes the extinction of plants and animals through the destruction of their natural habitats.

Sustainable wood is abundant though, and its scope as a building material is great, with floors, timber frames and wall panels just some of its many uses. Try to buy timber harvested from as close a source as possible in order to minimise energy consuming transportation. It is worth noting that British and Irish timbers are often not suitable for use in construction due to a lack of strength – a result of the rapid rate at which they grow.

20

Planning Permission and Building Regulations

A shake up in UK planning laws could make life much easier for home improvers if proposals to relax planning permission requirements get the go ahead.

At the time of publication a government white paper had been published outlining a more lenient approach to small home extensions and renovations. Among the changes proposed are a faster home improvement application and appeal service and the scrapping of planning permission for small projects that have no impact on neighbouring properties. The loosening of the laws is intended to take some of the burden off local planners who have seen such applications rise to around 330,000 per year. Also detailed in the paper are plans to charge for planning appeals, which are currently not subject to additional fees.

As this book went to print however, planning permission is still required in the UK if more than half the original amount of land surrounding the house is to be built upon, if the extension is higher than the highest point of the original house, if the volume of the house is increased by more than 15% (10% for properties within a conservation area) or if the volume of a house is increased by more than 115 cubic metres.

In Ireland, you can build, without planning permission, an extension to the rear of a house as long as it does not increase the original floor area of the house by more than 40 square metres and is not higher than the house. It is also required that at least 25 m2 of garden/land remains.

If permission is required, one option is to apply for Outline Planning Permission – this applies to permission in principal only and is valid for up to three years during which time you can submit your final drawings for Detailed Planning Permission (UK) or Consequent Planning Permission (ROI) if required. If however, you have drawn up your plans and are confident in them, a Detailed application can be made without prior Outline permission.

Remember that if your extension does require planning permission no building work can begin until full permission has been granted. Planners are cracking down on those who build without the official go-ahead and it is no longer acceptable to rely on getting retrospective or retention approval once the build is underway or complete. Those who do may face legal action or an order to demolish the building if the local authority deems it to be a blatant flouting of planning law.

It should be remembered that planning departments are supposed to favour new development, just as long as there is no reasonable cause for objection. If an application is refused there will be specific reasons for this which can in many cases be addressed and rectified. Your architect or house designer should be able to help you with minor amendments, although a planning appeal is the only option should your plans fundamentally breach local planning policy.

At present there is no cost for submitting a planning appeal in the UK, although moves to charge for this service have been outlined in the aforementioned government white paper. Planning appeals are made to the Office of the Deputy Prime Minister (ODPM) in England, the Scottish Executive in Scotland, the Planning Inspectorate (and in the case of large scale development, the National Assembly) in Wales, and the Department of the Environment (DOE) in Northern Ireland. The situation differs somewhat in the Republic of Ireland where planning appeals are subject to a fee and are dealt with by An Bord Pleanála.

If you are working with an architect or house designer they should be able to spot potential planning problem areas, but be aware of factors that could jeopardise the success of your application. Common grounds for planning refusal include:

Design: Designs that are out of keeping with the area can be refused if considered detrimental to the existing visual outlook.

Invasion of privacy: A window or balcony

that overlooks a neighbouring property can be seen as invasive. Be prepared for objections if you plan to use the roof of a new extension as a balcony area.

Off-street car parking: Depending on local planning policy there may be an issue as to the number of car parking spaces required if you extend your home. It may be the case that the local authority bases the provision of off-street car spaces on the number of bedrooms in a property. Another potential planning issue to be aware of concerns garage conversions or side extensions and where to park your vehicle if these areas are no longer available.

Scale: Planners may consider excessively large extensions as 'over-development' and refuse an application on this basis

Obviously, different planning authorities will have their own guidelines and it is impossible to produce a comprehensive list here so make sure you are aware of the planning restrictions in your area and have secured the necessary permission before starting your build. Booklets and other useful literature will be available at your local council office, as will The Local Development Plan, which details the planning policies of a particular area.

An important consideration when planning changes in and around the home are Restrictive Covenants (previous obligations imposed on the homeowner in the deeds of the property). Home buyers should be made aware of any such restrictions by their solicitor prior to purchasing a property, but be sure to check if unsure as they can restrict anything from building an extension to erecting a television aerial.

In addition to this, your plans will need to be submitted for Building Regulations approval. All extensions must adhere to building regulations, whether they require planning permission or not. These regulations are set out by the Government (updated in the UK in 2006) to ensure that at least the minimum

building, design, energy conservation and safety standards are met. Compliance usually rests with the person responsible for the build, such as the builder, should you hire one. Once approved, a

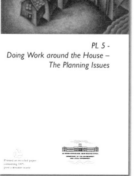

PL 5 -
Doing Work around the House –
The Planning Issues

THE PARTY WALL
etc. ACT 1996:

EXPLANATORY BOOKLET

completion certificate must be issued and kept safe in the event of a future house sale. It is recommended that homeowners retain final payment to their builder until they are in receipt of the completion certificate.

The majority of extension plans will require a full application Building Regulations submission. A Building Regulations application form must be supplied with full building plans to include construction methods, material types and a plan of the site location. You will also have to pay a fee at this stage, details of which can be obtained from your local council.

For further information consult the following:

PL5 Doing Work Around the House – The Planning Issues (ROI) www.environ.ie

UK residents can refer to the Government website www.planningportal.gov.uk

Homeowners in Northern Ireland should visit www.planningni.gov.uk for further information.

Hiring a Professional

Architects/House Designers

Adding on to your property may be a small scale build, but the effect it could have on the value of your home is huge. For this reason you may consider putting the plans in the hands of an architect or house designer.

Primarily, a design professional will be able to tell you from the off whether an extension is viable. They can design a space that suits your needs and prepare a submission to a planning department if permission is required. An architect/technician can ensure the plans contain all the required information and will know which plans are more likely to succeed in a given location.

They will also have a sound knowledge of building regulations, which will have to be met and approved, and health and safety legislation. Additional benefits might include construction industry contacts to engineers, builders and surveyors, and even project management should your budget stretch to it.

Choosing an architect or designer you feel comfortable with is hugely important – the enhancement of your home is in their hands and you must feel able to communicate with each other openly throughout the design process. The Royal Institute of British Architects (RIBA) recommends contacting two or three architects and requesting to see examples of previous work before making a decision. Contacting past clients for feedback is also suggested and is a good way to get an unbiased review of the service they provide.

Before commissioning an architect you must first clarify with them your budget and their capability to work within it. Secondly, and particularly if you have a specific design in mind, you must establish their flexibility regarding changes to drawings and incorporating your ideas. Handing over the reins to an architect or designer needn't mean relinquishing your own creative input, merely that your ideas can be channeled into a realistic plan –

one that suits your personal needs as well as being acceptable to planning authorities and harmonious to the existing house.

If design isn't your forte the experience of having an extension created especially with you in mind can be just as rewarding. You could also enlist an architect/design service to modify a stock plan, like the designs featured in this book, to your taste

When it comes to cost there are no hard and fast guidelines to go by due to the vast variation in project types and whether work is done on a percentage or hourly rate basis so this will have to be discussed with your architect/designer. Payment of these fees also varies depending on the size of your project. Be sure to define payment terms from the outset so these can be incorporated in your budget.

Some designers may offer to project manage the build if required, though there will be an additional charge for the service. If you are unable to be on site during the day, such a service could prove useful. Before bringing an architect or designer on board, there are a few points you should address first:

- Be clear in your mind about what you are trying to achieve and exactly what it will entail

- Couples/Business Partners should be in full agreement on what is required from the build before meeting with a designer

- Do you want input into the design or hand over full creative control to an architect/designer?

- How will your new extension enhance your lifestyle? If you work from home will it be used as an office? Maybe a larger dining area would be appropriate if you entertain regularly?

- If budget is an issue, are you thinking with space and cost efficiency in mind?

- What qualities are you looking for in an architect? You'll be working together closely and must feel confident enough to discuss any changes or concerns you may have.

- Do your research. Ask for previous examples of work and get feedback from past clients.

- Have you set your project a realistic budget? Are the architects you've
- contacted able to work within it?

- Who will be dealing most closely with the architect/designer?

- Are there certain materials, fittings etc you want to use? Are you thinking of a traditional or contemporary design?

- Can they do the job? Ask for proof of qualification/registration from designers and architects

A list of registered architects, plus further information on appointing the right one for your project, can be found on the RIBA website www.architecture.com

The professional body for architectural technologists is the Chartered Institute of Architectural Technologists at www.ciat.org.uk and the professional institute of Chartered Building Surveyors is RICS www.rics.org.uk

Those in the Republic of Ireland can visit the Royal Institute of the Architects of Ireland website at www.riai.ie

Builders

Unless you are planning a complete self-build, the likelihood is you'll be enlisting the help of a building company. In fact, if you are planning complex structural changes to your home, it is recommended to use the services of professionals to save time and money in the long run.

Tradespeople working on your project will be a fixture in your home for a substantial amount of time, making it essential to establish clear and open communications and a good working relationship from day one.

If you are employing the services of an architect or technician they should be able to recommend trusted builders. Ideally you should contact at least three companies

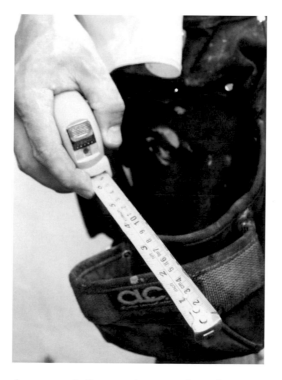

for a quotation and remember that the cheapest isn't necessarily the best. There are builders who specialise in the construction of extensions and it may be worth investigating these for their expertise in small scale builds.

In order to get a realistic quote, supply the companies you contact with as much

information as possible, including copies of detailed plans and full written specifications. Also check what their resulting quote covers – there are often unforeseen costs such as waste removal or scaffolding, so find out exactly what is and isn't included in the price. If you have asked for materials to be included make sure all prices for these are clearly broken down. Check that the builder is VAT registered and that the quote includes this.

There are a few main points that should be established about your builder before continuing with any reference checks such as:

- Membership of accredited trade organisation (e.g. National Guild of Mastercraftsmen in Ireland or Federation of Master Builders in the UK)

- Insurance cover – public liability

- Guarantees of work after completion

Another important detail to check before committing to a builder is whether they can realistically accommodate your extension into their schedule of works. Ask about other projects they have earmarked that are close to or coincide with your build and only agree to hire their services once you are sure your development will be given the required time and resources.

When checking the credentials of a prospective builder, first-hand references are invaluable.
Ask to see examples of previous work and if possible, contact past clients to clarify the following:

- Why they chose the builder in the first place (price, reputation etc)

- Level of communication between both parties

- That the project came in on time and budget

- That the site was well managed and health and safety standards were adhered to

- If there were any problems or faults with the work after completion

- That they are happy to recommend the builder to others

Once confident that you have found the right builder for the job, the next stage is getting it confirmed in writing. A contract clearly stating works to be carried out and payment installments, signed by both parties, is essential. Establish a timescale for the project and realistic finish date – whether you want to discuss the possibility of a penalty clause should work run over that date is up to you. Being able to refer to the written contract will be of reassurance should any problems arise during construction.
Before building begins make sure your site is ready and that toilet/kitchen facilities are available to workers. If you

cannot or don't want to allow access to your own rooms, provision for a portable toilet will have to be made in advance. Establish from the outset house rules – where the workers may or may not access the house, where materials and tools are

allowed to be stored etc. Make sure that any furniture or valued item near to the construction area is relocated, well-covered or even put into storage if you think it might be at risk of being damaged. You may also want to cover floors, carpets and walls in any areas used as walkways during the work. Your home should be left in a reasonably clean state after the build, as should any access routes in both your own and your neighbour's property.

Once work is underway, and assuming you have hired a good, reputable builder, you should be confident in their abilities to get on with the job in hand. Although it may be tempting, constantly checking on the progress of the build will slow things down, as will making lots of last minute changes. Obviously you will want to be kept aware of developments and may even help out with some of the work – just be willing to accept that the professional should know best and should be working with your best interests in mind.

That said, don't be talked into anything you are not certain about or rushed for an answer. If there is anything you are unsure of a good builder will be happy to talk through any concerns you might have. If you feel that aspects of the build are not going as you would wish, talk to your builder and explain your concerns - it will

be too late to do so at the end. Again, any changes to the original contract should be clearly established and factored into the overall costs at the time of occurrence and not added on as extras at the end of the build.

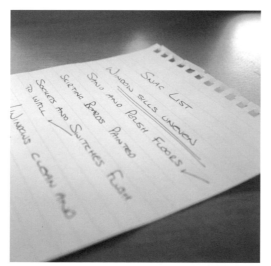

Once complete, thoroughly check through the work with the builder and address any issues you have there and then. Known as a 'Snag List' this offers a chance for the homeowner to highlight any aspect of the build they believe to be incomplete or not finished as agreed or according to the

plans. Make sure that the extension and site area are clean and that any paperwork/compliance certificates you require have been issued. If the work is guaranteed there should be no problem contacting the the builder at a later date if any subsequent problems arise. It has been known for homeowners to retain a percentage of the overall project cost until they are satisfied the completed work is of an acceptable standard.

Finally, when hiring a builder it is important to remember that not all arrive at your doorstep complete with lasso and spurs – the dodgy dealings of easily avoided 'cowboy' builders should not cloud your judgment when it comes to employing honest, legitimate professionals. Just be certain to base your searches on credible recommendations and carry out thorough background checks before signing any contracts.

A list of helpful websites on finding the right builder can be found on page 178

The Build

Self-build doesn't necessarily mean doing all the hard work yourself – if fact, when taking on complex structural changes to your home you should enlist the help of professionals to save time and money in the long run. Your involvement in the actual build can be as hands-on as your time and expertise allow, although even the most experienced home improver must leave installations of utilities such as gas and electrics to the pros. Alternatively you may decide to keep your hands clean and project manage instead having put together a team of qualified tradespeople to work on your project.

In cases where outside help is needed, do research carefully – get quotes from different builders/tradesmen and ask for references and contact details for former clients. (See Hiring A Professional: Builders on page 27)

It is vital to work out a definite payment schedule before any work starts. If you are employing a building company for the project do not pay for the whole job upfront - be aware that it is commonplace to pay a percentage of the total costs as each stage is completed. Such an arrangement is to the home owners advantage as it ensures work is carried out on time and allows for a steady cash-flow. Beware of builders asking for a deposit upfront – a reputable company will have the funds to begin a job and will have credit with builders' merchants for materials and equipment.

Pricing: Fix a price and pay for extras as they crop up, making sure that the expenses are carefully explained at the time. It is beneficial to both you and your builder to draw up a written agreement before work commences so both parties are aware of exactly what is expected. A reputable builder will be happy to commit to a written contract, but be wary of those reluctant to do so.

Do your homework: equip yourself with a good broad knowledge of building material costs, trade wages etc. Set a budget but be prepared to double it if necessary – try to cover yourself for every eventuality. If you work out a well considered budget, factoring in funds for unexpected extras, then it should not vary wildly from the builder's quote.

Designs don't always work in practice: sometimes what seems like a good idea might not go to plan and the design drawn up isn't necessarily functional in real life – you will have to put a certain amount of trust in the builder if he says it cannot be done, but don't be scared to ask for a full explanation why it can't.

Organisation is key: a delay of a few hours on site can have a knock-on effect which could end up costing you days or even weeks. If sub-contractors are being employed they may have other commitments as well as yours and may only be available for a certain amount of time. If you are in charge of buying materials, always confirm delivery times and order any extra stock as far in advance as you can.

Materials: think about the materials you are going to use for the build – are those used on the original house still available? If you are going for a contemporary extension, will the materials you plan to use blend in with or clash with what is already there? Making the wrong choice will result in an unsightly construction that will be expensive to put right. It is often the role of the builder to source materials although suggestions can be made if you have a good working relationship. Again, you can purchase your own materials, but you probably won't have access to trade contacts and discounted rates. Professional tools, equipment and commercial plant hire are costly, especially for those who aren't in the know.

Be mindful that delivery of different materials will affect the build timescale and that as many as possible should be sourced and delivered prior to the work starting. If you are importing materials from abroad allow for shipping costs and possible delivery delays – both of which will add to the overall expense.

Use old tiles from the back of the roof on a new front roof to continue the existing effect – the rear is not as noticeable and can be retiled to match. You should try to make your extension work in harmony with your existing home through your choice of materials and finishes.

Fixtures and Fittings: High end, expensive fittings and fixtures will look worthless if they are not installed correctly. It is a false economy to buy expensive doors, windows or floors and then try and put them in on the cheap. A botched job can't be covered up no matter how impressive the materials used. Installation of such features is not usually within the remit of the average DIYer and it is definitely a wise investment to have professionals fit them properly.

Alternative Accommodation: Even if it is on a small scale, building an extension will cause disruption to your daily life and it might be worth moving out while work is completed. Families with young children should consider this option due to the potential hazards on site.

Remember, for the duration of the build, your home will become a building site with all the disruption and safety hazards that entails. Not only will the building work impact on your home life, but if you live in a residential area, it will also affect those living nearby.

Establishing good communication with your neighbours can pave the way for a less stressful build. It can only be of benefit to have them on side as you may have to rely on their cordiality in terms of allowing access for machinery and vehicles, or if the use of emergency water or electricity supplies is sought.

It is not only the end product that will affect those living next to your property – they

on your site. By law these must be provided for workers if there are no other sanitation facilities available but they can be odourous and as a courtesy you should pre-warn those living adjacent to you.

The presence of trucks and delivery vehicles can cause an obstruction for others using the road and invariably there will be a certain amount of unavoidable noise so be sure to thoroughly discuss your plans and work schedule. If all parties are agreeable from the start it is less likely that objections will be raised at a later stage.

Health and Safety: The health and safety officer can shut down a site immediately if it is not up to safety standards – which in turn could cause long delays and result in the build not being completed on time. Such inspections are random and without warning so be aware of this. It is expected that the person in charge takes reasonable precautions to ensure the safety of both the site and those working on it. Hoardings or fencing should be erected if the site faces onto a public road or walkway and warning signs should be visible. There must always be a qualified first aider on site, as well as fire extinguishers and a properly stocked first aid box.

If young children are residing in the property during the build, clearly explain the potential dangers of the building site and be sure to secure the area to stop inquisitive youngsters getting in. Be vigilant during working hours and be sure that children aren't able to get into the building area or their hands on tools or machinery.

Insurance

It is the responsibility of the builder to ensure all sub-contractors are covered by insurance and the homeowner must check this is the case before any work begins. The building contractor needs insurance

too will experience some level of disruption during the course of the construction and you should be conscious of this. Ensure that building work is carried out within the appropriate hours and that no waste materials find their way onto the next door property. Another factor to consider is the provision of portable toilets

to cover the whole build including public liability and employer insurance. In the event of an accident where workers are not insured, the homeowner could be liable as owner of the site and the costs involved in an injury claim could prove exorbitant.

Time

If you intend to project manage or oversee the build, you will have to account for time off work in your budget. Alternatively you could hand responsibility over to the builder and check on the progress at pre-arranged times during the work. If you employ an architect at the design stage you may also be able to agree a deal with them to oversee the work, although this will incur further costs.

Financing a Home Extension

There are numerous options for securing the funds for an extension project. Equity Release loans allow homeowners to unlock money paid off their existing mortgage (the equity being the balance

between the value of the house and the outstanding amount owed) so that the costs can be absorbed into future mortgage repayments. Small scale builds may be funded by a personal loan, although interest rates on these are

usually high. Lenders can release up to 95% of a property's value in some cases. Talk to your mortgage lender about the options available before making any decisions.

Extensions

With a little imagination and some land to spare the scope to boost your living space without moving home is right there at your disposal.

Building on to a property has always proved a popular house expansion choice - planning permission is not usually a problem as long as size limitations are adhered to and the privacy of neighboring properties is not compromised. Extensions built to the rear of a property have long been the answer to space shortages, but what if such a development leaves you with inadequate garden space? Is there room to build on the side, or even the front of your home? If you want to bring a little light to your home, have you considered the more cost effective conservatory option? Obviously the choice of extension will be governed by the space available to build on, but are typically one of the following types:

Front Extensions
Designs on pages 42 - 53

Extensions to the front elevation of a property are almost always subject to planning control due to their obvious visual impact. If you are considering a build to front of your property it must be sympathetic to the surrounding

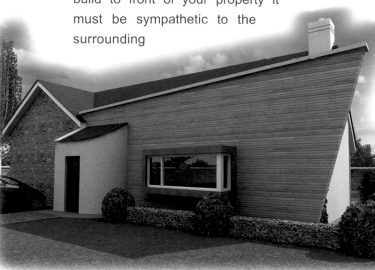

area and of an acceptable scale, proportion and design to even stand a chance of securing planning approval. Planning permission is needed for any front extension which stands closer to the road than the existing house does, unless the extension is more than 20m (67ft) from the boundary, and no part of the extension should come within two metres of any highway. A minimum distance of 21 metres should be kept between overlooking habitable windows on that of the new extension and those in existing properties.

Obviously care should be taken with the design of the extension to avoid detracting from the overall appearance of the building. This is of particular importance in the case of semi-detached or terraced properties as a badly designed extension will have a detrimental effect on adjoining properties.

Porches are normally dealt with more favorably and an application for a porch extension is more likely to be accepted where porches exist as a feature of other properties in the immediate vicinity of your home. However, if a new porch detracts from the appearance of neighbouring properties, consent may be refused. Any front extensions should be of minimal depth and bulk to ensure that they are not unduly prominent and do not detract from the local environment.

Side Extensions
Designs on pages 54 - 65

A side extension offers the opportunity for a two story build, although it can also be subject to planning objections due to prominence at the front of the house. The side extension can potentially make use of an area that might currently be under utilised – such as a side driveway or entrance to the back garden. This type of extension has become extremely popular in recent years due to soaring house prices

and lack of suitable new housing for those looking to upsize their living space. In fact, those lucky enough to have land on the side of a semi-detached or end of terrace home have great scope for property expansion.

If you are considering turning a garage or car-port into a side extension, you will have to make provision for the items currently housed there. Are you willing to leave your car exposed to the elements in return for more living space? Does the garage double-up as a tool shed or storage area? If so, you will have to factor in the relocation or disposal of anything presently stored there.

As a rule, planners do not like two-storey side extensions that stand level or forward of the front elevation of the house, and will not grant permission for any development that brings the property closer to the road. Avoid creating a terraced effect when adding to a semi-detached home by stepping the extension back from the front of the house.

If you are planning to build on the whole of the side area then access to the back door and garden will only be available via the main house. Aesthetic issues may arise in this situation if a lack of side or rear access means storing dustbins or recycling facilities at the front of the property.

If your plans include the use of a boundary wall you will be required to comply with the requirements of the Party Wall Act 1996. (For further information see Designing and Building Your Extension on page 15)

There may also be structural work involved, if for example you need to knock through or remove a wall to join the side extension to the existing house. In such situations it will be necessary to employ a structural engineer.

Skylights and roof windows are good methods of allowing natural light into a side extension, as is a large window to the rear looking out onto the garden.

Rear Extensions
Designs on pages 66 - 101

Building to the rear of a property is a popular extension option which takes advantage of available land provided by a back garden that may currently only be enjoyed during summer months.

In many cases, planning approval is straightforward as such developments do not impact on the overall aesthetic of a street or alter the outward appearance of neighbouring properties. However, planners are concerned that such additions should be in keeping with the original building and do specify common preferences in terms of design. For example, flat roofed 'box' style rear extensions are not generally favoured. Instead, pitched roofs with similar slates or tiles to the existing one are considered more visually pleasing. Also, the temptation to convert a flat roofed extension to accommodate a balcony is discouraged as it presents an infringement on the privacy of neighbouring homes.

Building at the back offers great scope for making the garden a feature of your home, giving the impression of bringing the outdoors in. Large glazed doors and ceiling to floor windows will provide an unobtrusive view to the natural surroundings – a living canvas so to speak. This type of design allows maximum light into a house and during winter months makes the garden

accessible, at least visually, at a time when it would normally be forgotten.

One consideration with a largely glazed construction is privacy. It will be necessary to carefully design your garden around the new structure to ensure your living area isn't too exposed – no one wants to feel they are on display in their own home. Strategic use of fencing, walls and natural barriers such as hedgerow and trees may have to be employed to combat this.

These also have the added benefit of creating a defensive shelter against the elements, reducing wind exposure and in turn boosting the energy efficiency of your home.

The rear extension is a great option for those who enjoy entertaining - a free-flowing extension that opens up into the garden is perfect for al-fresco dining and parties.

Conservatories and Sunrooms
Designs on pages 122 - 143

Let's throw some light on the subject of conservatories and sunrooms. Firstly, the difference between the two is not terribly distinct. There do not seem to be any hard and fast characteristics to separate them – although both are heavily glazed structures normally built on to an existing property in order to add extra space and light. The word 'sunroom' is an American term for what we on this side of the Atlantic would refer to as a conservatory or glazed extension, so in that respect there is no real difference at all, although we are more likely to associate a sunroom with a brick built extension with a solid, insulated roof rather than the metal, glass and glazed roof style of a typical traditional conservatory.

Even specialist companies seem unable to clarify what constitutes either a conservatory or sunroom, and many websites on the subject feature widely varying definitions – ultimately though both will open up your home to the surrounding landscape, helping to bring the outside in and giving you a front row seat to watch the changing seasons.

Design wise, the conservatory/sunroom has come a long way since the pot plant and wicker look of years gone by. Modern constructions are more likely to find use as a dining room, kitchen, children's playroom, or even a home spa.

One style of glazed extension is that of the 'patio room', which consists of a new structure being built upon an existing patio or decked area for added support. Generally these are intended just as the name suggests, an enclosed patio to be used in warmer months. In contrast, modern conservatories and sunrooms are better insulated, include heating and cooling systems and are suitable for year-round use. Be sure your conservatory specialist or designer is absolutely clear on the type you want.

If you intend your sunroom/conservatory to be a year-round, fully functioning extension to your home, there are some considerations to take into account in terms of design and budget, including adequate insulation, ventilation and access to electricity and water supplies (depending on the use of the room). The type of glass used in the construction of the extension is also important and nowadays should comprise of the energy efficient Low E variety, which should protect you from the sun's harmful UV rays while allowing heat and light in.

In terms of energy efficiency, wooden window frames, while generally more costly, are a better option than metal frames. Also, be aware of additional costs for blinds and window coverings (particularly for glazed roofs) which often need to be custom made and rarely come cheap.

As a rule, a conservatory/sunroom won't add a huge amount to the value of your home unless it adds to the actual living space, such as providing a new kitchen or living room. However, you will make your money back as long as the extension is constructed to a good standard and works in harmony with the original house.

Mexlib Designs ltd
David Quinn

Front Extension

This originally small dormer house has nearly doubled in size thanks to a new two-storey entrance area. The new accommodation includes a separate dining area linked to a new sitting room, playroom, two bedrooms and master ensuite bedroom.

Before

Dominic Whoriskey Architect
Dominic Whorisky

Roof Extension

Originally a single storey bungalow, this extension and renovation project provides a large family home with balcony. This is achieved by raising the roof to provide a wall plate dormer roof with projection, allowing a balcony to be incorporated.

Roger Parry & Partners
Paul Middleton

Side Extension

Utilizing the side of the house and garden area to add a two story extension giving a garage and utility room on the ground floor and a large bedroom on the first floor

Before

Ivory Architects
Stephen Macartney

Front Extension

A total renovation of a 19th century farmhouse that was extended in the 50's. A timber clad entrance 'box' creates a new entrance and sitting area to take advantage of spectacular views to the front. The internal layout has been reconfigured to create a double height gallery family room and allows the originally dark, low ceiling dwelling to be flooded with daylight.

Mexlib Designs ltd
David Quinn

Rear Extension

This extension is designed to utilize existing space and avail of the scenic views with an upstairs open plan living room. The original sitting room was cut-off from the kitchen and unused but now they are directly linked. Upstairs also accommodates a guest bedroom and large storage area. The curved roofs, large glazed areas and natural stone cladding modernize this bungalow.

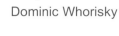

Dominic Whoriskey Architect
Dominic Whorisky

Side Extension

Originally a two bedroom semi, this design creates three bedrooms and separate living space. The gable has been extended outwards to provide an additional first floor bedroom with ensuite and living room with conservatory to the ground floor. The front porch is included to create a feature entrance.

Before

Mezzanine Architects & Management
Brian Mulvey

Side Extension

Created on land to the side of this end of terrace property, this double storey extension is stepped back from the original frontage and features a lower roof, which softens the visual impact and makes this a subtle addition to the house.

55

Before

Mexlib Designs ltd
David Quinn

Side Extension

Continuing from the previous design, this is a larger version boasting three large bedrooms and room for a mini gym. On the ground floor the extension is split level, into the dining and living room. The dining area is open plan with the kitchen and a laundry room has been added.

Mexlib Designs ltd

David Quinn

Side Extension

A large extension to a small house makes it a more modern, functional home. The front of the existing house has been converted into a large living area with high ceilings and a conservatory area just off it. The house also has a kitchen/dining area, three bedrooms, two ensuites, a bathroom and a utility room.

Dominic Whoriskey Architect
Dominic Whorisky

Rear & Side Extension

This contemporary extension to a semi-detached dwelling brought the living space into the garden. The large sliding doors allow light to enter the living space.

Before

Before

Mezzanine Architects & Management

Brian Mulvey

Side, Roof & Rear Extension

This house had already been extended to the rear and had no room to the side, leaving the only option left, to build up. A steel frame has been incorporated in the roof to maximise space and the roof design matches neighbouring houses at the front.

Mexlib Designs ltd
David Quinn

Side Extension

This house required an extra living room and large garage. The garage is positioned to one side of the house and has an attached lobby so that it can be entered from dwelling. The new lounge features high ceilings with oak beams and the existing kitchen and dining room have been redesigned to work better with the new open plan lounge.

Dominic Whoriskey Architect

Dominic Whorisky

Rear & Side Extension

This extension transforms the kitchen into a more family user space and accommodates a master bedroom with a superb external view .

Roger Parry & Partners
Paul Middleton

Rear Extension

A rear extension to provide a garage, lobby and utility room on the ground floor and a master bedroom and ensuite above.

Roger Parry & Partners
Paul Middleton

Rear Extension

A rear extension that provides a snooker room and extended kitchen.
The flat roof above was used to create a patio area off the master bedroom.

Mexlib Designs ltd
David Quinn

Rear Extension

Utilizing the southern area of the house a larger kitchen/dining area has been relocated to gain better light during the day. This large extension also provides three extra bedrooms, a large office space, TV room, utility room and two shower rooms.

Mexlib Designs ltd
David Quinn

Rear Extension

Utilizing the southern area of the house a larger kitchen/dining area has been relocated to gain better light during the day. This large extension also provides three extra bedrooms, a large office space, TV room, utility room and two shower rooms.

Mezzanine Architects & Management

Brian Mulvey

Rear Extension

This is a 40sqm extension to the rear of a detached four bedroom house comprising a large open room that connects to the existing kitchen. The room has a great view and captures the evening sun, making it the hub of the house.

Mezzanine Architects & Management

Brian Mulvey

Rear Extension

A large one room extension to the rear of a property. It has minimum impact on the existing dwelling due to its connection via a glass knuckle. The room is extremely light and airy with its vaulted ceiling and floor to ceiling glass.

Ivory Architects
Stephen Macartney

Rear Extension

Originally two farm worker cottages within a terrace of four, the rear extension provides a light filled family room and a first floor bridge link from the original dwelling to the new master bedroom - formed around an external courtyard. The result is a light, bright and warm fusion of contemporary style balanced with the intimacy of the original cottage.

Ivory Architects

Stephen Macartney

Rear Extension

This single storey timber clad sun room extends the kitchen to form a bright family / dining area linked into the kitchen. The rear doors open out into the garden and the space relates to the adjacent lounge which opens into the garden to form a social summer space.

Rear Extension

A south-facing, rear extension, this structure has been stepped lower to accommodate a large master bedroom above the new kitchen/dining area. On the ground floor an ensuite bedroom has been added. The bathroom area has doubled in size and the old kitchen/dining area has been redesigned into a large lounge area.

Mexlib Designs ltd

David Quinn

Before

Stage 1

Stage 2

Stage 3

Rear Extension

A large detached family home renovated to integrate small rooms into larger and flowing family spaces. A glazed gabled extension allows the kitchen and family room to relate to the garden and provide a light, bright, social space that the house previously lacked.

Ivory Architects

Stephen Macartney

Mezzanine Architects & Management

Brian Mulvey

Rear Extension

This terraced house has been remodelled to create more space for today's living while maintaining as much green as possible. The internal court yard allows for light back into the existing dwelling and the glazed section allows a light connection. The grass roof can be enjoyed via the first floor.

Roger Parry & Partners
Paul Middleton

Rear Extension

Height restrictions and budget constraints meant a simple reworking of the layout to achieve a useable family area.

Roger Parry & Partners
Paul Middleton

Bungalow Renovation & Extension

A tired and dated 1960's dormer bungalow is transformed with a large extension and a redesigned interior.

Rear Extension

| **Ivory Architects**
| Stephen Macartney

A bungalow with attic bedrooms was given a two storey timber and glass 'garden room' and master bedroom linked to the existing house with a glass corridor to maximise light penetration into the house.

Leslie R Hutt
John Braid ACIAT

Rear Extension

Though this modern extension may be substantial it is kept within the width of the existing stone cottage thus retaining the traditional appearance from the street. Large terraces and balconies exploit views and provide privacy.

Mezzanine Architects & Management

Brian Mulvey

Rear Extension

A large passive designed extension to a single storey terrace house.

Mezzanine Architects & Management

Brian Mulvey

Rear Extension

A typical single storey terrace house, a large extension has been added to the rear to capture the evening sun and give a modern feel to a traditional house.

Mezzanine Architects & Management

Brian Mulvey

Rear Extension

A sunroom that would not interfere with the sunlight in the existing kitchen was the brief for this design. Placing the sunroom at an angle to the existing dwelling allowed this and also creates a sun trap to the rear. At the other end of the house the garage was connected via a glass knuckle.

Mexlib Designs ltd
David Quinn

Rear Extension

This extension adds character to the front and increases the living area of this house. A large glazed area has been added at ground level to make use of the south facing aspect. At the rear of the house an extra area accommodates a mini gym.

JP Timber Construction
John Jobling-Purser

Rear Extension

A completely new structure designed to compliment a Georgian house. Double glazed six panel windows of Georgian design and four panelled sliding doors feature.

The roof at the rear incorporates a flat sun terrace accessed from the second floor window and supported on two sandstone columns within the conservatory. An internal plinth under the windows incorporates trickle irrigation planters.

JP Timber Construction

John Jobling-Purser

Rear Extension

This simple design provides office space to a 1970's bungalow. The frame is of Scot's Pine clad in teak, to match the windows of the original building.

JP Timber Construction

John Jobling-Purser

Rear Extension

A new addition to a Victorian house, this extension was designed to house plants. It has a standard shallow hipped roof to avoid interference with the second floor window. Double doors with white painted internal and external timbers feature.

JP Timber Construction

John Jobling-Purser

Rear Extension

A large conservatory built on the site of a Georgian house, this design was required to compliment the house and gardens and function as a 60-seater restaurant. The structure incorporates a lantern roof with vertical openings for ventilation.

JP Timber Construction
John Jobling-Purser

Rear Extension

This conservatory replaces an existing Victorian conservatory that had fallen into disrepair. The new structure copies the original design, only with new features such as double glazing, anti glare tinted glazed roof and opening sky lights for ventilation. The structure is accessed from the terrace by double doors.

Conversions

Unlike an extension, a conversion allows the homeowner to create extra living space without forgoing available land. This makes it an ideal option for those looking to utilise a redundant space in or around the home, be it an attic, basement, garage, barn or outbuilding.

A conversion may be required to accommodate a growing family or simply to facilitate lifestyle choices – a converted barn or outbuilding could become the perfect studio or workshop, offering seclusion from the main home. Similarly, a converted basement, with its solid walls and generally good sound proofing would suit a range of uses, from a home cinema, gym, or music rehearsal room.

Basement and attic conversions are not necessarily subject to the same stringent planning restrictions and so can offer a certain amount of creativity in terms of design. Similarly, an attic conversion can offer enormous potential in terms of expanding your living space – and with

proper planning budgets both options could come in as a cheaper alternative to building a whole new structure if the space already exists.

If the option is open to you, making use of an empty or unused space will not only increase your living/recreation area, but done well will boost the value of your property.

Attic

A popular option for many homeowners with attic space is to extend up to the top of the house - and given the light, solar and cost benefits it's easy to see why.

Attic conversions make great use of unused space, and because the windows look directly out to the sky, they offer light drenched areas suitable for a range of uses, be it a spare bedroom or studio. There is an almost hideaway quality offered from an attic room - a bolt hole in which to escape from the rest of the

house. The sanctuary it affords is also well suited for use as a relaxation area, reading room or study.

Creating a rooftop retreat is generally not as costly or disruptive as building a new external extension from scratch. The main expenses will derive from creating access into the attic, paneling walls, laying down floorboards, and window and heating installation.

Another attractive aspect of the attic conversion is that planning permission should be a straight forward affair, providing there are no major external changes as a result.

Attics come in all shapes and sizes and many taper down at each end to follow the natural shape of the roof. In order for the room to be considered habitable, planning regulations rule that two thirds of it must be at a height of at least 8ft from ceiling to floor. In addition to this, your conversion must have a structurally strong floor, proper fire escapes and safe stair access to the floor below and be properly heat insulated and sound proofed.

Access is probably the biggest consideration when planning an attic conversion – will your current landing accommodate a staircase, or will you have to divide up an existing bedroom to make more space? Pull-down ladder stairs are not suitable for habitable loft areas, although they will suffice if the attic room is for storage purposes only.

Building regulations dictate that there must be a minimum 80 inch space between every stair and the ceiling – something to be aware of if the staircase ends in an attic with a sloping roof overhead. Staircase design will also be determined by the space available – a straight staircase will obviously require more floor space to support it, while spiral staircases, despite being visually interesting and space saving, can cause problems for children and elderly relatives and won't allow for large objects, such as furniture, to be transported via them.

In terms of heating, the attic area should benefit from heat produced on the floors below rising up. Don't waste this

economical side-effect by not properly insulating the attic conversion. Rooftop level skylights and windows are usually

exposed to the elements with no natural shelter, and as such are susceptible to drafts and frosts in the winter.

Basement

Perhaps least obvious of all house extension options is the basement

conversion, this despite offering fantastic utilisation of space often ignored.

Recently an increasing number of homeowners have been digging deeper for sought-after living space; indeed, going underground can satisfy a number of extension criteria. A basement conversion can however throw up numerous building challenges, particularly if there is no underground area already in place. It is possible to extend below ground level without an existing basement in place, but the space will need to be dug out by hand and high costs and significant disruption will be inevitable.

Planning consent should not prove as problematic as no land is being built on (although as always, restrictions vary depending on the planning authority so it is essential to check before starting any work.) That said; the creation of lightwells will call for permission, particularly at the front of a property, as this involves the excavation of gardens and or driveways and can have a visual impact on the general streetscape - a concern already raised by a number of planning authorities in London.

Without planning restrictions, the size of the extension could potentially be as large if not larger than the ground floor of the house - a factor that has undoubtedly prompted the current boom of basement conversions in densely populated towns or anywhere where land and space is limited.

It is important that you discuss plans with neighbours and draw up a party wall agreement if the conversion affects their foundations and walls. You will also be liable for surveyor fees on their behalf under the Party Wall Act (UK only).

Modern basement conversions are an infinitely more attractive prospect than the image of a dark, dank cellar used only to store redundant household knickknacks. Instead, an inspired design can open up a whole new dimension to your home – be it

a multi-function family entertainment room, home cinema, self contained living quarters - even an indoor swimming pool!

In many ways, expanding downstairs could prove more practical than heading up – floors will be more solid than those in an attic making it ideal for heavy duty uses such as a home gym or kitchen.

Taking into account the work and costs

involved, converting an existing basement is the ideal solution. However, a growing number of specialist companies can dig out the required space although it will be more expensive and disruptive and it should be expected that such work will take at least three months to complete.

Damp should not be a problem providing the basement conversion is properly damp-proofed and well ventilated. Building regulations require a natural air flow which can be achieved via an open staircase to the floor above or through an external air pipe.

Access to natural light is essential in making a basement conversion a pleasant, habitable place, and can be achieved by creating light wells around the site or installing a glass paved area overhead to act as a transparent roof and an unusual and contemporary patio area above ground. Light can also be provided by opening up the basement to the floor above to create an open stairwell.

Barns & Outbuildings

Should you be in the possession of such, a disued barn or similar outbuilding is an obvious, if somewhat costly, candidate for conversion.

Although the basic structure is likely to be in place, the cost of bringing an old, neglected building up to modern Building Regulation standards should not be underestimated. However, the expense of such a project pays back many times over in the sense of achievement to be had in restoring, preserving and making functional once more a piece of the past.

The extent of work involved in a barn or outbuilding conversion depends on a number of factors including the age and construction of the building, its current state of repair and the proposed use for it after conversion. Inevitably structural work will have to be carried out to make the building acceptable for habitable purposes– the main areas of attention here would be

making secure the roof and ceilings, and replacing any damaged and rotting timbers. Barns and outbuildings that have been left neglected for a long period are likely to have come under attack by insects and various forms of rot and fungi, possibly rendering parts of the construction unstable and dangerous. A

detailed survey should always be undertaken before drawing up any plans to establish whether or not a renovation is even possible.

In terms of planning permission, designs that are sympathetic to the original

building, and that restore rather than revamp are more likely to be approved. Wherever possible try and retain original materials such as roof tiles, timber and bricks, and if replacement materials are absolutely necessary, try to source these locally, as the originals are likely to have been. Intended use is also a factor in securing planning permission for barn and outbuilding conversions - common policy on this seeming to favour business rather than residential use. (By the very nature of the conversion, it is likely the application will be made to planners based in a rural location, who would be looking to promote the economy of the area). Grants may also be available to those planning a barn conversion for eventual use in a business capacity.

Of course, you may wish to create a country retreat within the grounds of your own home for family and guests. (Although it is possible that your barn or outbuilding may already be host to guests of the feathered and winged variety – the habitats of owls and bats are protected and if they are present this too will be a planning obstacle). In the case of barns specifically it should be remembered that such buildings were originally designed with livestock or crops in mind, not the home comforts we would expect from a dwelling. In many cases, barn doors will have to be changed and extra windows installed (if indeed any exist in the first place). These are substantial changes not only in terms of cost, but also from a planning perspective, bearing in mind that approval is more likely to be granted if the original character of the building remains intact. For example, rooflights would be a more acceptable solution than dormer windows, and small and few windows at ground level should be considered.

Be sure to consult with your local planning officer as to what is and isn't acceptable before going ahead with any plans.

Garage

As it entails, broadly speaking, the conversion of an existing 'room', turning your garage into a livable area of the home should be a relatively straightforward proposition.

In many cases, a garage conversion is exempt from planning permission as long

as no additional volume is created, (although you should always check with the local planning authority before undertaking any work). If you park your vehicle in the front garden, or have designated on-street parking, your garage

might only be providing an expensive storage solution at present and if this is the case, integrating the space into your home is a sound decision in terms of functionality and property value. Garage conversions can facilitate a range of uses – from extending kitchens and living rooms, to adding on a whole new dimension, such as an extra bedroom or playroom for children.

Depending on the type of garage, a conversion can be as simple a matter as creating a suitable construction in place of the original garage door. This is most likely to consist of a wall and window, with access into the new room from the main house. Obviously any work carried out must adhere to Building Regulations as with any construction work. Other points to consider when converting a garage to a habitable area are means of access and escape (in the event of a fire or other emergency) proper ventilation and drainage provisions should the conversion house a bathroom or toilet.

Mezzanine Architects & Management

Brian Mulvey

Garage Conversion

This mews is inspired by the need for nature in an urban setting. An existing tree and a manmade waterfall have been incorporated into the house, showing even in an urban jungle nature can still be all around.

Roger Parry & Partners
Paul Middleton

House Renovation & Extension

Side and rear extensions have helped to
produce a spacious family home.

Mezzanine Architects & Management

Brian Mulvey

Cottage Restoration & Extension

A rear extension to an existing country cottage. The original features of the existing cottage remain while the extension has a more modern feel - a contrast of old and new. The front door has been repositioned and the dwelling reorientated to achieve a passive design.

Leslie R Hutt

John Braid ACIAT

Outbuilding Conversion/Extension

This site originally consisted of a single storey stone building which was used as a stable/storage area. The stable was converted to provide a work/office area and extended with a new two storey residence. Large areas of glazing are incorporated into the front elevation to exploit southerly orientation and views.

129

Leslie R Hutt

John Braid ACIAT

Barn Conversion

This conversion is of a derelict listed barn with a brief to form a modern residence whilst maintaining the character of the building. All existing openings have been utilised and new window openings kept to a minimum.

Mezzanine Architects & Management
Brian Mulvey

Garage Conversion

At the other end of the
house to the kitchen and
sunroom, the garage was
connected via a glass
knuckle ideal for a home
office

Roger Parry & Partners
Paul Middleton

Garage Conversion

A simple garage which is part of a
major restoration of a fabulous six
bedroom, three storey house.

Leslie R Hutt

John Braid ACIAT

Outbuilding Conversion/Extension

This conversion takes an existing derelict stone building and forms a new residence. New large openings, sun lounge extension and large rooflights exploit a southerly aspect.

Dominic Whoriskey Architect
Dominic Whorisky

Cottage Restoration & Extension

A dilapidated stone built cottage
restored and transformed with a
modern extension in keeping
with the traditional style.

Leslie R Hutt
John Braid ACIAT

Cottage Restoration & Extension

A ruined ancient stone cottage is restored to its former glory with generous glazing and a new extension to the rear to create a modern holiday cottage.

Roger Parry & Partners
Paul Middleton

Barn Conversion

Perfect as a guesthouse, this extension provides an ideal annexe that feels separate from the house.

Redesigning your Garden

If you are constructing an extension to the front, side and particularly rear of your home then it is likely that your garden will need to be redesigned in some way.

If land surrounding your home is used for access or as a storage area for materials during the course of the build, scaffolding and machinery will almost certainly damage lawns so keep this in mind as you will have to figure in costs for rectifying your garden once the work is complete. Reworking your garden to fit in with a new extension is a good opportunity to breathe life into a tired or underused outdoor area and make it a further extension of your home.

This section is intended as a general guide to planning your grounds once an external extension has been built, and while it is impossible to cover the vast scope of plant types and gardening techniques here, readers will find a list of informative publications and websites on those subjects at the back of this book.

The integration of existing natural features wherever possible is a good, not to mention cost effective idea, but where to find inspiration for your new and improved garden?

Gardening programs, exhibitions, books and the internet offer a wealth of ideas, and observing other people's gardens can conjure up ideas of what might and might not work in yours.

Think big and visit the gardens of some of the UK and Ireland's stunning stately homes and historic houses. Your garden may not lend itself to the scale of such grand designs but there's no more inspiring sight to ignite a creative spark.

Having established what you want from your garden the next step is the actual design. This process can be as hands-on

as you decide as there are a number of options at this stage.

For a fee, an experienced garden designer will talk through your requirements and come up with a proposal, schedule of works and estimated cost. Using these plans you can either hire a landscape gardener to complete the work, or engage the garden designer to project manage a contractor.

Alternatively you could try your hand at design online – there are a number of websites that allow you to create a to-scale virtual garden, with different plant, furniture and feature options such as this 3D design tool at w w w . b b c . c o . u k / gardening/htbg2/virtual_garden

Finally, there is the more traditional DIY approach. This will require an accurate scale drawing of your site which your architect

or surveyor should be able to provide. Be sure to mark in existing features that you plan to keep and note any large items outside your boundary when putting your plans together.

Deciding exactly what your garden will be

used for is an important aspect of the design process – decking or a largely paved area is perfect for those inclined to outdoor entertaining, while a soft, grassy area is best for small children to enjoy. Creating different sections depending on your requirements not only makes for a more visually interesting garden but also allows your land to become more functional. Vegetable patches and herb gardens not only look (and smell!) rustic and homely, but are also functional in providing healthy, home-grown food. Low maintenance Japanese style 'zen' gardens are an ideal option for those looking to create an oasis of calm with minimum upkeep - consisting mainly of rock, stone, sand and accompanied perhaps by the gentle babbling of a water feature. Think carefully about how and when your garden will be used and think of it as a further extension of your home rather than incidental to it.

Preparing the garden site

Before work can begin you will need to clear the site of debris such as stones, bricks, cement and timber. The soil should be cleared to a depth of between 250 & 300mm (10-12") with all removed items disposed of off-site and responsibly.

If there is a notable presence of weeds these should be eradicated before proceeding any further. If you plan on digging them up, do a little research first. It is worth noting that some types prosper by having their roots broken up, leading to more weeds and more work in the long run.

It is also a good idea to test your soil for its PH level (acidity or alkalinity) prior to digging and turning. DIY testing kits are available from most garden centres. A loam soil (a mix of sand, silt or clay, and organic matter) is generally considered to be the best type as it is suitable for the

widest range of plants, but do check that the plants you intend to use are compatible with the soil type. As an extra boost to get the most from your soil, try mixing in some organic matter such as fresh bagged mushroom compost or manure. This will work wonders for flowerbed and vegetable patches.

Picking Your Plants

There may be plants or shrubs that you want to keep from your existing garden to replant once construction is complete. If you are going for a complete redesign check beforehand that any new plants you have in mind suit the soil type and location. Investigate which ones flourish in neighbouring gardens and incorporate plants and shrubs native to the area for a feeling of consistency and the benefit of local wildlife. Pay particular attention to colour to avoid unsightly clashes and overcome the 'busy' look by restricting the number of varieties and repeat plant instead. Climate is also a major consideration and will have a huge impact on the success of your garden. Observe the movement of the sun throughout the day to identify sunny and shady areas (taking into consideration how your new extension will affect this) and plant accordingly. Check for prevailing winds as some plants are susceptible to wind damage.

Hard Features

Patios, decking, paths, garden sheds and green houses etc may already be installed in your garden and will possibly need to be moved or removed to accommodate the extension. After construction these features can be replaced or new ones added in the new space – this being the perfect chance for a complete garden makeover.

Plant covered trellis and carved arbors add dimension and are useful tools to 'frame' a particularly attractive section of garden, while climbing plants and timber frames can be used to hide less appealing features such as composting bins or water tanks.

Outdoor lighting gives you the option to enjoy your garden at night, be it for entertaining or relaxing, with solar powered lights being the most energy efficient choice. Be considerate of neighbours when installing lighting features and aim for a welcoming glow rather than an airport runway. In terms of visual embellishment it's hard to improve on Mother Nature's handiwork, but there's no reason not to enhance this with some garden 'art'. Anything from traditional stone statuettes to modern, abstract sculpture goes, depending on taste.

Soft Features

Bear in mind that large soft features such as trees and bushes will continue to grow in size over the years. This presents a number of implications including longer shadows cast over your garden and extension, more space being taken up, views being obscured and large roots which can rupture foundations, walls, paths and patios. Special attention will have to be paid to these issues and regular maintenance is essential.

If the lawn has been severely damaged during construction work, you might consider re-laying it with turf.

Where to plant flowers, shrubs and herbs is a matter of personal choice – flowers beds, plants boxes, pots, urns and hanging baskets can all make attractive displays and are a great option for small basement gardens where space is limited. When marking out plant and flowerbeds, keep in mind areas of shadow and light and also to the drainage needs of your plants. Be aware of seasonal cycles – what time of year do they flower? Will they

provide colour in winter? If your extension is glazed and the garden is a prominent visual feature you will want to ensure this view is enticing all year round. If you are a novice to gardening, you'll certainly benefit from expert knowledge. An array of informative books on the subject can be found at your local library and bookshop. Designing your extension and garden in conjunction with each other not only makes for a more harmonious finish but also blends your new extension in with its surrounds in the minimum amount of time. As with the main construction design, research and planning are vital when it comes to the garden. Thinking ahead is extremely important. It is nature's job to grow and evolve - the garden you plant today will be quite different after a year or two and will change dramatically as time goes by. Don't try to pack in too much. It may be tempting to cover every inch of bare soil with flowers and plants at first, but you need to give them space to breathe, mature and grow into your garden.

If you find your fingers aren't the slightest shade of green you should go for a garden that requires minimal upkeep – making use of elements such as decking, bark chippings and pot based plants rather than free growing plants and lawns. Remember, too much to take care of and not enough time will quickly result in an unkempt garden that will detract from the look of your home.

Thermal Regulations

Although we might not realise it, our homes significantly contribute to levels of harmful carbon dioxide emissions and energy waste - in fact around 40 per cent of Europe's total CO_2 emissions are a by product of domestic energy use.

Regulations have been introduced in the UK and Ireland to reduce these damaging effects and anyone planning on extending or renovating their home will have to ensure their new build complies with the new requirements.

In June 2006, the amended Part L1A of the Building Regulations (England and Wales) was created in response to global climate change, and in particular to reduce the level of 'greenhouse gases' of which buildings account for almost half in the UK. Similarly, the Irish government recently set in motion the first phase of implementing the Building Energy Rating system as part of the EU Energy Performance of Buildings Directive.

Limiting heat loss, temperature control and owner awareness of operating and maintaining energy conscious services are among requirements that must be fulfilled to ensure an adequate standard of fuel and power

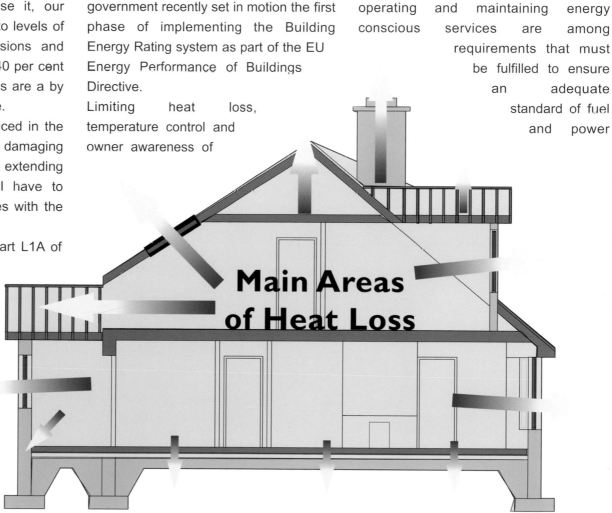

Main Areas of Heat Loss

Image courtesy of Xtratherm

conservation in all new dwellings.

It is hoped that more stringent regulations will promote innovative approaches to clean, renewable heating and power sources which in turn will replace finite fossil fuels and curb the detrimental effect their burning has on the natural environment. It is intended that a 20% reduction of carbon emissions will be achieved in the UK by 2010 as a result of the new regulations.

What do these changes mean?

UK

Since the changes were introduced in the UK in April 2006, new homes require a Dwelling Emission Rate (DER), a rating based on the estimated annual emissions per square metre caused by space and water heating, domestic hot water, ventilation and lighting. The predicted rating must come in under a government set Target Emission Rate (TER) for it to comply with the new regulations.

Performance standards are set for the building as a whole, rather than for construction and service elements, and more rigorous pressure testing on air-tightness is called for prior to completion.

In order to help construction professionals, developers and self builders meet the requirements demanded by the new standards, a more flexible method of compliance regarding the DER has been developed - replacing the three applicable in 2002 (Elemental Method, Target U-

Value Method and Carbon Index Method). Compliance can be met through various factors including improvements in construction methods, air-tightness and improved materials.

To achieve compliance, five criteria under Part L1A must be met:

1. The predicted carbon dioxide emissions (DER) must be no greater than the Target Emission Rate (TER). Data to enable the production of an Energy Performance Certificate must be provided.

2. Defined limits on design flexibility, building fabric and service performance must not be exceeded. This is intended to discourage inappropriate trade-off, for example buildings with poor insulation standards offset by renewable energy systems with uncertain service lives.

3. Excessive solar gains must be prevented in order to avoid overheating in summer. The aim here being to counter

excessive internal temperatures and reduce the need for air conditioning and other cooling systems.

4. The performance of the dwelling is consistent with the DER, specific requirements regarding the quality of the construction and commissioning must be achieved including air-pressure tests and commissioning.

5. Provisions for energy efficient operation of the dwelling are put in place. Satisfactory information on efficient energy use must be provided to occupiers. The energy rating of the building should also be displayed in a prominent area.

Both the DER and TER are calculated using the latest version of the Standard Assessment Procedure - SAP 2005. This methodology is used to assess energy consumption in new dwellings. (All new buildings must have a SAP rating, although there is no minimum standard they must attain).

Again, based on estimated annual energy use including ventilation, heating, lighting and hot water, SAP 2005 works on a scale system where 1 rates as poor and 100 excellent - the higher the number, the lower the carbon emitted.

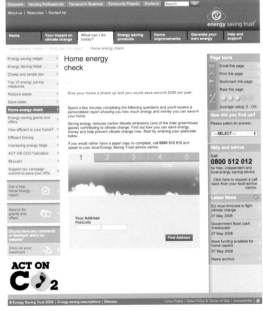

www.energysavingtrust.org.uk

The TER is the minimum energy performance for new dwellings approved by the Secretary of State. It is based on a

hypothetical dwelling and estimated using SAP calculations based on the same size and dimensions but encompassing reference values for building fabric and heating. It is expressed in terms of the mass of CO_2, in units of kg per m2 of floor area per year emitted. In addition, carbon dioxide emissions from properties which run on fuels other than gas are further multiplied by the fuel factor and so will affect the TER.

Recommendations in the revised report advocate the use of more environmentally sound energy methods such as solar heated hot water, photovoltaic power, bio-fuels (wood and oil blends), combined heat and power systems and heat pumps, the use of which can make substantial and cost-effective contributions to meeting the TER. Further information on these systems can be found in the Low and Zero Carbon Energy Sources Strategic Guide (May 2006) at www.planningportal.gov.uk where the full version of Part L1A Building Regulations is also available to download.

Republic of Ireland

As of January 2007, all new dwellings in the Republic of Ireland must undergo an energy audit before they can be sold or let. The carbon dioxide emissions a property creates are calculated using the Dwellings Energy Assessment Procedure (DEAP) which is used to assess compliance with Part L (Conservation of Fuel and Energy) of the Irish Building Regulations.

The procedure follows the framework set out in the EU Energy Performance of Buildings Directive (EPBD) and draws heavily on the calculation methods used by the UK's SAP system. The carbon output of a dwelling is established by calculating its Carbon Dioxide Emission Rate (CDER) with the corresponding Maximum Permitted Carbon Dioxide Emission rate (MPCDER), expressed in units of kg Co2 per square metre per annum. The main aim of the DEAP is to limit harmful emissions associated with domestic energy uses such as space and water heating, ventilation and lighting. Limiting heat loss, maximising heat gain and controlling the output of heating and water systems are top of the agenda in terms of keeping a home energy friendly.

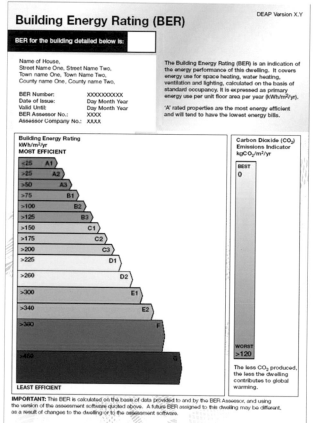

On completion of an audit, a Building Energy Rating (BER) label – similar to that used to signify the energy efficiency of household electrical appliances – will be awarded, along with a BER Advisory Report with recommendations on improving the building's energy performance.

The audits will identify exactly how, where and why domestic energy is used, where energy savings can be made, and will eventually be applicable to all dwellings, not just new builds.

A full, updated version of the Dwellings Energy Assessment Procedure has been published by Sustainable Energy Ireland and is available at www.sei.ie

Environmental Impact and Energy Efficiency

If you're making the effort to improve your home it's a good time to consider improving your 'carbon footprint' at the same time.

Environmental impact and energy efficiency can sometimes be overlooked when designing an extension. Your small scale build may seem like a drop in the ocean in terms of the carbon emissions it creates, but it will nevertheless have an impact on the greater environment.

Looking at the big picture, it is estimated that 50 per cent of the world's pollution comes directly and indirectly from dwellings. For that reason it's worth looking at ways to reduce the carbon effect for the benefit of both your surroundings and your pocket.

The high rate of household carbon emissions are caused by a number of factors - the fuel we burn to heat, the chemicals we use to clean, and the energy used to make our house building materials. For example the aggregate used in concrete has to be quarried,

crushed, graded and transported to where the concrete is mixed, loaded into another truck and delivered to your site. This process requires diesel or electricity for the machines and vehicles, which is most probably generated through the burning of fossil fuels.

At all stages of the building process there are opportunities to minimise the impact your house will have on the environment such as; the positioning of the extension in

relation to the sun and the elements of weather, the amount of concrete or timber required to build your design, where these products come from and how they are made, the level of insulation in your walls, windows and roof and the type of heating system used.

Think about using locally sourced, renewable materials where possible to ensure a green build with limited environmental impact.

Materials and Construction
Building materials and their impact

The production of building materials is responsible for about one-tenth of energy consumption and CO_2 emissions in the UK and so it is recommended that you investigate material options and the implications of the ones you use. How are the materials made? Where and what are their future energy benefits? Comparing building materials and products in this way, along with their cost and ease of use, will allow you to choose the best for you and the environment - for example buying UK or European timber means there is far less transportation involved than buying from North or South America.

Assessing a material's impact needs consideration of several factors (Roaf 2003):

- The energy required to produce the material
- The CO_2 emissions resulting from the material's manufacture

The impact on the local environment resulting from the extraction of the material (e.g. quarry pit, wood taken from the forest, oil spill from an oil well etc)

The toxicity of the material

The transportation of the material during its manufacture and delivery to the site

The degree of pollution resulting from the material at the end of its useful life

Embodied energy is the amount of energy a material or product uses in its production and requires to be kept in working order. This can include everything from the mining of the raw material to the transportation by sea, air and road to where it becomes a finished product, then on again to your site and its eventual integration as part of your home.

Calculating the embodied energy can get quite detailed, for example the process of pressing chipboard will require a certain amount of delivered electricity, and that

Photo-Voltai

Local Ston

Rain Water Storage

Geo-T

Eco House

Panels)

Solar Water Heater

Mechanical Heat Recovery & Ventilation System

Well Insulated Hot Tank

Commercial Wind Turbine

ouble or riple Glazing

Porch for additional heat retention

Underfloor Heating with Thermal Insulation Below

Timber from sustainable forests

Eco-Concrete

Domestic Water Turbine

Biomass Boiler

ource

electricity may have been generated by burning coal or oil. This level of calculation would involve too much detail for most home builders. However asking a few questions and choosing materials and products on environmental grounds rather than price or convenience, can have a big impact. If we all do our bit it soon adds up to a significant difference.

Renewable energy sources

With the recognised change in climate conditions and global warming brought on by the burning of fossil fuels it is important we do what we can to limit these damaging effects. Environmental studies suggest our dependence on such fuels has had a detrimental effect on the environment and as such we must try to reduce our energy usage. Deriving energy from environment friendly, renewable sources benefits not only the individual household but to the wider global environment.

Although there are no exact figures as to the quantities of coal, oil and gas reserves left on the planet, oil, upon which we are dependent on for many everyday uses, is expected to show signs of serious decline by 2020, if not sooner. Gas is expected to run out sometime between 2050 and 2070 and coal in 2200.

Designing your home, and any extension to it, to be less dependent on fossil fuels is a smart move in terms of future proofing and to help reduce carbon emissions.

The world consumes 82million barrels of oil/ per day or 1,952,381 metric tonnes (1.5b ltrs)

How environmentally friendly and energy efficient your home is will have a direct impact on you and your family in the decades to come.

In respect of a new extension, the benefits of a well insulated building fitted with energy efficient appliances and heating systems are obvious - reduced fuel bills and a better standard of living, as your home will be easier to heat and sustain warmth at less cost.

Solar Energy

Heating

Solar Passive Heating means heating areas direct from the sun. A house facing directly south or within 15° and having 50% of the vertical surface high quality double or triple glazed, allows sunlight in and little heat out. The light is best when falling on a concrete wall, and/or the floor (slate or dark coloured tiles) to enable it to become heat energy. These surfaces slowly heat up during the day and similar to a storage heater, gradually release this heat after the energy supply has ceased. Sun rooms, conservatories and other heavily

Thermal vacuum tubes

glazed extensions are designed to harness the sun's energy, warming quickly. To maximise these benefits it is important to close curtains after the sun has set to keep as much heat in as possible.

Water

There are various methods of heating water with the sun's visible and infrared rays including:

Thermal vacuum tubes – the tubing is well insulated by a vacuum (similar to a thermos flask), making this type of system very efficient. It is easy for the contents to gain heat but very hard to lose it. Water is passed through the collector and fed into a hot water tank and can be heated further by an emersion or boiler system.

Computerised tracking collectors – both of the above can be fitted to a tracking system that simply rotates the panel so it is facing the sun at the optimum angle and tilt at all times. Any financial savings may be compromised with this option due to installation costs.

Flat radiator format – relatively easy to install on an exterior surface but unable to absorb a high percentage of the energy falling on them and may lose more energy than it gains in cold temperatures

Solar Power

This is a simple process of converting the sun's light energy into electrical energy through photovoltaic (PV) panels, very similar to a solar calculator, except on a far grander scale. There are a variety of panel types producing differing levels of power per square metre, with costs reflecting this. PV panels covering an area of 10 square metres in an average home could generate up to 30 per cent of power. Full sustainability may require many panels and may also present problems in terms of storing power surplus for later use.

If in the process of renovating your home, it may be worth making provision for PV tiles as a replacement material for the roof. If you are planning on using solar power this will reduce the cost of paying for both these and roof tiles. Otherwise, solar panels can be bolted on over existing roof tiles.

Construction and positioning
Solar Benefits

If your extension faces south it will be possible to maximise the amount of heat energy or passive solar energy from the sun, although not all locations are suited to south facing positions.

www.estif.org

Absorbing the sun's rays during winter months will greatly reduce your heating bills and CO2 emissions, but position alone is not the only way to improve the energy efficiency of your extension. There are three steps to consider - getting the energy into the house, absorbing this energy for gradual release when the sun has set and controlling it through the variations of our climate.

Before deciding on design and methods of generating solar power you will have to consider; the strength of the sun at different times of the year, location of the sun at different times of the year in relation to the site, how much of the sun's heat a building needs at different times of the year for the comfort of the occupants and energy storage capacity.

Wind Power

This is another example of how a natural resource can become a great power

www.awea.org

source. With the ability to create up to 2.5KW, domestic wind turbines can contribute significantly to your renewable energy. As a guide to usage, 1KW = 1000watts. Most light bulbs use 60watts/hr, microwaves 700watts/hr. As with generating electricity from solar panels, this source of power will not yet supply 100% of your power needs but could make a significant contribution. Be aware that the construction of a domestic wind turbine will require planning permission in most instances.

Biomass Energy

This is the use of any naturally occurring material such as wood, plant matter, cow slurry, and most waste material that is available on a renewable basis. These materials are burnt, contained for gasification or fired with fossil fuels. The most commonly used for domestic use is wood which when growing* absorbs as much CO2 as when burnt, making it an ideal renewable energy source. For burning in modern stoves, the wood comes in the form of pellets. These stoves are sealed units and their efficiency levels are between 75 and 90%, considerably better than a traditional open fire with an efficiency level of just 20% and its remaining heat energy going up the chimney.

Once a tree reaches maturity and its growth slows it absorbs less CO2 and adversely gives out less oxygen.

Grants and Initiatives

The Department of Trade and Industry (DTI) launched the Low Carbon Buildings Programme in 2006 to provide grants for microgeneration technologies for householders in the UK. Managed by the Energy Saving Trust, these grants are available to those installing renewable energy systems, such as solar photovoltaics, small wind and hydro turbines, and solar thermal hot water systems. For further information log onto www.est.org.uk

In the Republic of Ireland, the Greener House Scheme provides grants to homeowners looking to install renewable energy systems such as solar panels, ground, water and air source heat pumps and wood/chip pellet boilers and stoves – see www.sei.ie for more information.

When choosing timber, consider types approved by The Forestry Stewardship Council (FSC) which promotes the responsible management of forests worldwide.

Insulation and Areas of Heat Loss

Many houses have air leaks, thermal

Wood pellets for a biomass boiler

bridges and insufficient insulation. Before thinking about using environmentally friendly and renewable energies it is important to first have an energy efficient house with heat losses minimised from the roof, walls, floors and windows, as well as any air leakages from vents and extractor outlets.

A closed entrance porch and back door that accesses the main house via a utility room or conservatory create air-locks which prevent internal warm air escaping through open doors. These air-lock areas also preheat the cooler fresh air before it enters the house. Using the utility room as a place to wash and dry clothes will stop the moisture released leading to condensation and the potential for mould.

Thermal bridges are parts of the house made of materials that conduct heat and connect the interior to the exterior, such as concrete or steel lintels, steel ties, window frames or any solid masonry bridging the inside walls to the outside walls. The warmth within the house passes to the

porch - air lock

cooler outside via these bridges.

To remedy common heat loss issues the following products are recommended:

Nylon wall ties
Split lintels above windows and doors where structurally suitable
Timber frame or aluminium windows with thermal spaces or seals; e.g. the aluminium does not run continuous from the inside to the outside of the frame
Double or triple glazed windows with a high insulation value

Timber sub frame instead of returning brick work around walls and doors

Effective insulation and minimal areas of heat loss will reduce the energy required to heat your home and maximise heat retention, keeping it warmer for longer. Eco-friendly types of insulation are now widely available and can be made from materials including recycled newspaper, hemp and lambs wool.

Ventilation

The control and quantity of ventilation will have an impact on your health and comfort in both winter and summer. Ventilation affects heating and cooling costs and helps prevent mould in areas of

and must comply with building regulations. The following options are viable from a regulatory, cost and environmental

standard to any home, but often overlooked is how the windows open, size of the opening sections and how secure the home is when they are open. Being able to open a small window within a frame can allow for an amount of ventilation on a winter's day and with adequate locks, can be left open while you are out. Alternatively, in summer you will require window to open as wide as possible in a frame to keep the house cool and fresh throughout the day.

Moisture build up from insufficient ventilation

condensation. There are various ways to ventilate a home, some are mandatory

perspective:
Windows that open are an obvious

Passive Stack Ventilation This system depends on the warm stale air rising. An exit pipe is required in areas generating the highest quantities of stale air, such as the kitchen and bathroom. It will generate a continuous background airflow by sucking fresh air in from other rooms. These air inlets and outlets can have humidity controls to increase or decrease airflow depending on the levels of moisture. Such passive systems have the advantage of very few moving parts, minimal maintenance and energy consumption

Trickle Vent This kind of vent is usually seen as slots in window frames and is generally required by building regulations unless a whole house ventilation system is being installed. If using just trickle vents, extractor fans will need to be installed in areas of high moisture creation such as the kitchen, bathrooms and utility room. Fitting the fans with humidity sensors will reduce their energy consumption.

Mechanical Ventilation and Heat Recovery (MVHR) systems work best with well insulated houses where only the incoming fresh air requires heating. The system passes the outgoing stale air over a heat exchanger, which then provides the heat

for the incoming fresh air. A good system can create the majority of heating required for incoming air with some coming from a

Mechanical Ventilation and Heat Recovery (MVHR) system

small heating element within the system. The fan fitted needs to use as little energy

as possible if its cost is to be covered by the energy savings.

Light

Bringing efficient natural light into your extension/home is relatively simple providing all rooms have at least one window. Quantity, quality and distribution of the available light contribute to the temperature and functionality of a given room. It is estimated that a window area equal to 10% of a room's floor area will give a daylight factor of 1, which should be the absolute minimum, for an average room of 10 -14 m2 a window area of 15% will give a daylight factor of 2 and 25% area a factor of 3.

The daylight factor is based on the amount of daylight falling on a horizontal surface of a room as a percentage of the daylight falling on a horizontal surface outside. (For further information and an example of this see www.sustainabilityworks.gov.uk).

Long narrow rooms with one window in an end wall will suffer from glare near the window and dim light at the farther points.

The best light can be achieved by having windows on two sides, which maximises the amount of direct light coming into the room at different times of the day. Better again is to install sky or roof lights where possible.

For areas that do not receive adequate light during daylight hours, supplement what does come through with good quality artificial light that doesn't create areas of heavy contrast or glare. From an environmental perspective long life eco bulbs should be used for their long life and energy saving qualities.

Noise

Depending on the location of your home there may be unwanted sounds from road, rail or air traffic and perhaps

Window areas of a room 48m² (A) 2.4m² 5%, (B) 4.8m² 10%, (C) 7.2m² 15%, (D) 12m² 25%

even the natural surroundings.

There are also factors to consider regarding disturbing noises within the home. The most notable being uncarpeted staircases, hollow dry lined walls and wooden floors with no sound absorption between the boards and joists. The following suggestions may also help to combat potential sources of environmental noise:

- Ensure there are no cracks or other air paths for sound to pass through
- Keep to high standards of construction and detailing Create external barriers to muffle noise
- Specify high-quality windows with controlled ventilation
- Use sound absorbing materials in cavity walls

Water Conservation

It is estimated that 65% of water usage is

domestic. It is also estimated that with a little modification the average household

could reduce its usage by up to 50%.

The water used in your home has to be collected in a reservoir, treated and

pumped to your house. (In some cases you may have your own water source or a share in a well). The process requires energy and this energy will likely require the burning of fuel, which in turn leads to CO_2 emissions. The difference one household makes by using water more conservatively may not be huge, but if ten thousand homes did the same, the difference would be vast. During the year when water shortages occur being more water conscious can also help alleviate this problem.

There is also the financial benefit of reduced water usage which will be apparent in your electricity or gas bills. A simple measure to keep costs down can be made simply by using a shower instead of a bath, and indeed in the type of shower you install. Appliances such as washing machines and dishwashers come with energy efficiency ratings, letting you know which use the least water and power – a benefit to the environment and good news in terms of running costs.

Compost Bin

Domestic Waste

UK households produce around 30 million tonnes of rubbish per year. The issue of domestic waste disposal is of major importance as landfills run out and those still active or closed leak poisonous effluents into ground water and release greenhouse gases into the atmosphere. How you deal with your waste has significant environmental and financial impacts and you should allow sufficient space for effective refuse and recycling management.

Councils across the UK and Ireland are gradually supporting the recycling effort and many residents are now required to dispose of their waste accordingly. This should be divided into organic, glass, metal, plastics, non-recyclables and any other suitable category. As some of these types build up and/or decompose faster than others, suitable storage areas will be needed. For example, taking glass to a bottle bank may only be required once a month but organic and non-recyclable waste would need to be disposed of every few days to avoid unsavoury odours.

A compost heap is ideal for the disposal of organic and garden waste, which contributes to around 50% of the average household's total yearly waste.

Compost heaps require approximately 2 – 3 square metres of space, a consideration that will factor heavily when building a rear extension on an existing back garden. Composting not only cuts down on waste but provides nutrient packed food for your garden.

Integrating the recycling ethic into your house/extension design will benefit the property and your day to day convenience. Factor in those areas

for refuse storage, bearing in mind room for separate waste bins. Try to combat the unappealing look of bins being left around

the side of the house and avoid the prospect of piles of recyclables in the shed

or utility room. A great facilitator to recycling is convenience. If your refuse disposal strategy is well conceived, it makes the business of rubbish much more attractive. Make sure there are enough bins, bags or boxes close to hand so there is no excuse not to separate the waste.

Construction waste

Many common construction materials can be recycled and used again in various forms after they cease to be part of a home. If you are knocking through or demolishing a part of your house to make way for an extension, bear in mind that the waste produced could still prove to be useful.

Domestic recycling plants are unlikely to accept construction waste however so, when hiring a skip, enquire as to operator's arrangements for reusing or recycling the contents as some will separate and sort them for recycling. Choosing a company based on their recycling strategy is a positive step in terms of keeping your build environmentally friendly.

Aluminium which may be found in old door or window frames is 100% recyclable and has numerous uses. Recycling aluminium requires only 5% of the energy and produces only 5% of the CO_2 emissions as manufacturing it from scratch.
Wood/Timber can be reprocessed and manufactured as chipboard board or horticultural mulch.
Concrete can be crushed and recycled as aggregate for new concrete or road base and fill.
Glass can be recycled many times without losing clarity or quality and is used in construction for windows and doors. It can also be crushed and used as aggregate for concrete.
Carpet may not be recycled at a recycling plant, but can be put to good use in a

garden as mulch, or as a weed barrier. Bricks and Tiles can often be reused as they are if in good condition or form part of a new feature such as a path or barbeque. Rubble created by knocking down walls or other demolition can be used in a patio foundation.
Plastics can be granulated and reused to make new plastic products and include: High Density Poly Ethylene (H D P) :

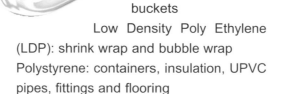

rubbish bins and buckets
Low Density Poly Ethylene (LDP): shrink wrap and bubble wrap
Polystyrene: containers, insulation, UPVC pipes, fittings and flooring

Practical Energy Saving Tips

Turning your thermostat down by one degree can reduce your energy consumption by up to 10%, with the same reduction in greenhouse gas emissions.

Secure a shelf or window board over radiators that are under a window to prevent heat loss.

Sealing drafts saves up to 25% of household heat loss. A brush or seal on exterior doors and covered keyholes and letterboxes will help eliminate drafts.

Open fires can lose up to 85% energy content through the chimney – wood stove fires are a much more efficient option, proving to be between 70-90% effective.

Installing double glazing and good insulation are long-term cost effective ways to reduce heating bills and household carbon emissions.

Keep doors closed between rooms so that heat does not escape into unheated areas.

Over 60% of a home's energy

consumption is accounted for by heating water – swap baths for showers and be considerate in your hot water usage.

Switch to energy saving compact fluorescent lamps (CFL's) which use only

a fifth of the energy of conventional light bulbs.

Aluminium foil placed behind radiators conserves heat as the foil reflects warmth back into the room. Special radiator foil can be found in DIY stores but normal tin

foil works almost as well

Don't turn up the thermostat if you're feeling chilly – put on a jumper or extra layer of warm clothing instead.

Whenever possible wash clothes at 30°C to save energy and help to reduce CO2 emissions. Detergents designed to work at low temperatures are now available.

Don't leave electrical items on standby or needlessly on charge.

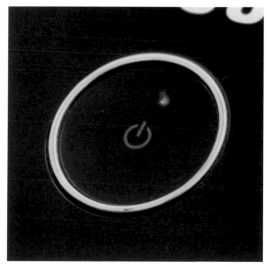

Harvest rain-water for use in the garden rather than wasting treated tap water.

Featured Architects
& Designers' Contact Details

Dominic Whoriskey & Associates
Dominic Whoriskey

Main Street
Newtowncunningham
Co.Donegal, Ireland

P/F: +353 (0)74 9156996

dominicwhoriskey@eircom.net

Mexlib Designs ltd
David Quinn

4 Sheeaun Park, Athenry
Co.Galway, Ireland

P: +353 (0)91 850532
F: +353 (0)91 850533

plans@mexlibdesigns.com
www.mexlibdesigns.com

Leslie R Hutt
John Braid ACIAT

3 View Place, Inverness
Inverness-shire, IV2 4SA
Scotland

+44 (0)1463 235566

LHuttArchitect@btinternet.com

JP Timber Construction
John Jobling-Purser

Rosnastraw
Tinahely
Co.Wicklow
Ireland

P: +353 (0)402 34853
M: +353 (0)87 2647300

Roger Parry & Partners
Paul Middleton

Hogstow Hall, Minsterley,
Shrewsbury,
Shropshire, SY5 0HZ
England

P: +44 (0)1743 791336
F: +44 (0)1743 792770

mail@rogerparry.net
www.rogerparry.net

Ivory Architects
Stephen Macartney

66 Rawbrae Road
Whitehead, BT38 9SZ
N. Ireland

P: +44 (0)28 93 353725

ivoryarchitects@aol.com

Mezzanine Architects & Management
Brian Mulvey

No. 30 Merrion st Upper
Dublin 2
Ireland

P: +353 (0)1 6787879
F: +353 (0)16787889

Palace St
Drogheda
Louth
Ireland

P: +353 (0)41 9819902

Dublin st
Ballyjamesduff
Cavan
Ireland

P: +353 (0)49 8545861
F: +353 (0)49 8545868

22 Ferry St
Isle of Dogs
London, E14 3DT
Engand

Phone: +44 (0)700 341 8688

mezzanine.architects@gmail.com
www.mezzanine.ie

Websites & Recommended Reading

Websites

Ireland

Design
www.riai.ie (Royal Institute of Architects of Ireland)
www.garden.ie
www.glda.ie (Garden and Landscape Designers Association)

Planning & Building Regulations
www.oasis.gov.ie
www.environ.ie
www.scs.ie

Building
www.selfbuild.ie
www.iaosb.com (Irish Association of Self Builders)
www.thebuildingsite.net
www.onlinetradesmen.com
www.nationalguild.ie (National Guild of Mastercraftsmen)

Environmental
www.sei.ie
www.enfo.ie

Useful Information
www.iavi.ie (Irish Auctioneers and Valuers Institute)
www.constructireland.ie

UK

Design
www.architecture.com
www.biat.org.uk (Chartered Institute of Architectural Technologists)
www.thegardenplanner.co.uk

Planning & Regulations
www.planningportal.gov.uk
www.buildingcontrol-ni.com
www.onlineplanningoffices.co.uk

Building
www.house-extension.co.uk
www.selfbuildland.co.uk/home-extension.htm
www.myworkman.co.uk
www.findabuilder.co.uk
www.uk-builder.com
http://www.building-contract.co.uk/building-contract-package.htm
www.aecb.net (Association of Environment Conscious Builders)

Environmental
www.raceagainstwaste.com
www.lowcarbonbuildings.org.uk
www.wasteonline.org.uk
www.sundancerenewables.org.uk
www.greenphase.com
www.wasteonline.org.uk

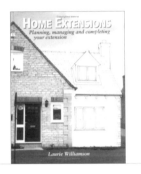

Home Extensions: *Planning, Managing and Completing Your Extension*
Laurie Williamson
The Crowood Press Ltd;
Reissue edition
ISBN: 1861262914

Home Extension Manual: *The Step-by-step Guide to Planning, Managing and Building a Project*
Ian Rock
Haynes Group (2007)
ISBN: 1844253570

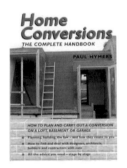

Home Conversions: *The Complete Handbook*
Paul Hymers
New Holland Publishers Ltd
ISBN: 1843303523

The Housebuilder's Bible
7th Edition
Mark Brinkley
Ovolo
ISBN: 0954867440

House Plus: *Imaginative Ideas for Extending Your Home*
Phyllis Richardson
Thames & Hudson Ltd
ISBN: 0500342113

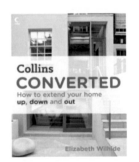

Converted: *How to Extend Your Home Up, Down and Out*
Elizabeth Wilhide
HarperCollins Publishers
ISBN13: 9780007229406

**Spon's House Improvement
Price Book**
Brian Spain
Taylor & Francis
1 edition (2000)
ISBN: 0419241507

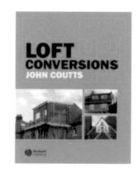

Loft Conversions
John Coutts
Blackwell Publishing Ltd
ISBN13: 9781405130431

Home Extensions: *The Complete
Handbook*
Paul Hymers
New Holland Publishers Ltd
ISBN13: 9781843303732

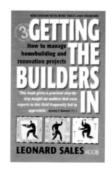

Getting the Builders in:
*How to Manage Homebuilding and
Renovation Projects*
Leonard John Sales
How To Books Ltd;
3Rev Ed edition
ISBN13: 9781845282332

**Converting to an Eco-friendly
Home** - *The Complete Handbook*
Paul Hymers
New Holland Publishers Ltd
ISBN10: 1845374061

**The Property Makeover Price
Guide:** *Organising and Budgeting for
Home Improvers and Developers*
Various
Building Cost Information Service
ISBN: 978-1904829522